STONE SOUP

Illustrated by Sharron O'Neil

Adapted by Mary Rowitz

Louis Weber, C.E.O.
Publications International, Ltd.
7373 North Cicero Avenue
Lincolnwood, Illinois 60646

Manufactured in U.S.A.

ISBN: 0-7853-1918-2

PUBLICATIONS INTERNATIONAL, LTD.
Stories to Grow On is a trademark of Publications International, Ltd.

A hungry traveler had been roaming the countryside and hadn't had a good meal in days.

Off in the distance, the traveler spotted a village. "I'm bound to find someone there who will share a meal with me," the traveler said to himself.

As the traveler rushed to the village, he tripped over a stone in the road. The stone was not like any the traveler had ever seen. It was perfectly smooth and oval in shape. The traveler decided to keep it. "You never know when a stone like this might come in handy," he said.

Then the traveler headed to the lovely village. His empty stomach grumbled as he walked.

One house the traveler came to was very quiet. All the doors and windows were closed, and the shades were drawn. He wondered if there was anyone home. Finally a maid appeared in the doorway. "Can you spare some food?" the traveler asked. "I am very hungry."

"I'm sorry, but I have only a few potatoes," the maid said, "not enough to spare or share. Why don't you try my neighbor next door?"

"I already have," said the traveler, "but he was very grumpy and just slammed the door. It looks like finding some food in this village will be more difficult than I thought." Still the hungry traveler refused to give up.

The traveler went everywhere in the village, but no one had enough food to spare or share. One house had only cabbage, the next had only carrots, and a third had only salt and pepper.

Since there was no food to be found, the hungry traveler decided to leave. As he rested under a tree, the traveler looked back at the quiet little town. "It's a shame," he thought, "such a nice village and such a beautiful day, but nobody is outdoors talking or playing."

Then the traveler reached in his bag and took out the stone he found earlier that day. The hungry traveler was admiring the stone when he had a brilliant idea!

The traveler ran back to the village and shouted, "Come out of your houses, everybody! I have a magic stone that will give us enough food to spare and share!" One by one, the curious villagers peeked out of their doors and windows.

The grumpy villager who slammed the door on the traveler earlier looked out of his window and shouted, "What's all the racket about?"

"Come help me make a pot of delicious stone soup," said the traveler.

The maid stepped out of her house as two children ran up to the traveler. "Is that your stomach I hear growling?" one child asked.

"Yes, I am very hungry," said the other.

"Does anybody have a kettle?" the traveler asked.

"I've got one," said the big, grumpy villager, "but I don't think it will do any good."

Most of the villagers were excited, but some were doubtful. "Do you really believe he can make soup from a stone?" asked one young lady.

"I guess we'll find out soon," said another.

The grumpy villager brought out a large kettle and placed it on a pile of sticks for the fire. "Are you sure that your magic stone will make enough soup to spare and share?" he asked.

"Yes," said the traveler, "there will be plenty."

The traveler placed the stone into the kettle of water and began to stir. Then he tasted the soup. "Not bad," he said, "but it could use a little salt and pepper."

"I've got some," said one of the young ladies, and she went home to get it.

"Perhaps the soup would taste even better if I shared my potatoes," the maid suggested.

"Yes, that's a great idea," said the traveler.

The young lady returned and sprinkled her salt and pepper into the kettle. Then the maid dropped in her potatoes. The traveler stirred and tasted the stone soup a second time. The villagers watched him with anticipation.

"This is very good, but it would taste even better with some carrots and cabbage," said the traveler. Then a young boy ran home to get some carrots, and a girl ran home to get cabbage.

By now, everyone was having so much fun that they forgot how hungry they were. Even the big, grumpy villager was no longer grumpy. "Let's make this meal a party!" he shouted.

The girl returned with the cabbage, and the boy soon followed with his carrots. "Just think, a huge kettle of soup made from a magic stone," said the boy. "I can't wait to try it!"

Finally the traveler announced that the stone soup was ready. He filled the bowls, and the villagers began to eat. Afterward there was plenty left over. "There's enough to spare and share!" said the young lady.

The villagers were so happy after dinner that they didn't want the evening to end. They started playing music and dancing. The village was alive with chatter and laughter.

"I didn't know you could play the banjo," said the maid.

"I didn't know you could play the washboard."

"There was a lot we didn't know until the traveler came along," replied the maid.

The next morning, the traveler said good-bye to his new friends. It was time for him to leave. "I want you to have this," he said as he gave the smooth stone to the villagers. "Now you'll always be able to make stone soup together, and you'll never be hungry or sad or grumpy again." The villagers hugged the traveler and told him to visit their town again some day.

As the traveler headed out of the village, he stumbled over another stone in the road. He picked it up and admired its dark, jagged edges. "You never know when a stone like this might come in handy," he said as he placed it in his bag.

Cooperation

Cooperation means working with others to do things that need doing. The hungry traveler used his stone to show the villagers how to cooperate. When the traveler came to town, each of the villagers had a little bit of food but not enough for an entire meal. The traveler helped the villagers work together to make a delicious soup.

Cooperation can make difficult things easy, and it can be lots of fun. The villagers learned that it's easy to make friends when you work together.